Contents

Key

* easy

** medium

*** difficult

Caribbean food

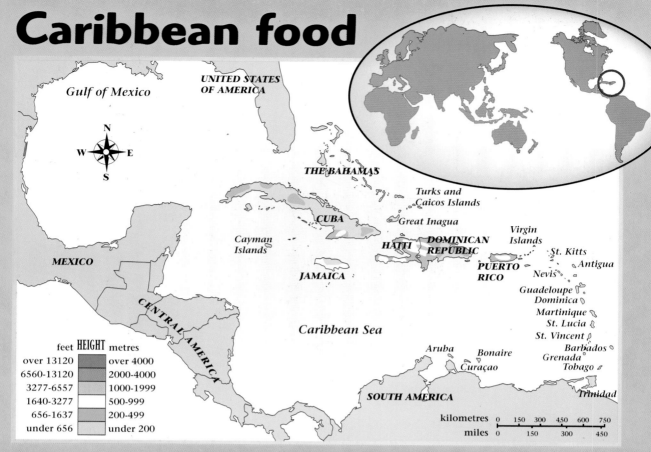

The map shows height in feet and metres:

feet	HEIGHT	metres
over 13120		over 4000
6560-13120		2000-4000
3277-6557		1000-1999
1640-3277		500-999
656-1637		200-499
under 656		under 200

The Caribbean is a large area off the east coast of Central America. It is made up of many different countries. There are hundreds of islands in the Caribbean. Some of them are very large; others are so small that no one lives on them.

In the past

The Caribbean islands were originally inhabited by groups of American Indians, first by the Arawaks and then the Caribs. These people grew maize, sweet potatoes and peppers, and caught fish.

In the 15th century, European explorers began to travel to the Caribbean. People from Spain, the UK, France and Holland settled in the islands. They began to grow sugar on huge farms called plantations. The settlers realised that they needed people to work on these plantations, so they captured men, women and children from Africa, and brought them across to the

A World of Recipes

The Caribbean

Julie McCulloch

www.heinemann.co.uk
Visit our website to find out more information about **Heinemann Library** books.

To order:
☎ Phone 44 (0) 1865 888066
▤ Send a fax to 44 (0) 1865 314091
▭ Visit the Heinemann Bookshop at www.heinemann.co.uk to browse our catalogue and order online.

First published in Great Britain by Heinemann Library, Halley Court, Jordan Hill, Oxford OX2 8EJ, a division of Reed Educational and Professional Publishing Ltd. Heinemann is a registered trademark of Reed Educational & Professional Publishing Limited.

OXFORD MELBOURNE AUCKLAND JOHANNESBURG BLANTYRE
GABORONE IBADAN PORTSMOUTH NH (USA) CHICAGO

Designed by Tinstar Design (www.tinstar.co.uk)
Illustrations by Nicholas Beresford-Davies
Originated by Dot Gradations
Printed by Wing King Tong in Hong Kong.

ISBN 0 431 11704 7   (hardback)   ISBN 0 431 11711 X   (paperback)
05 04 03 02   06 05 04 03 02
10 9 8 7 6 5 4 3 2   10 9 8 7 6 5 4 3 2 1

British Library Cataloguing in Publication Data
McCulloch, Julie
    Caribbean. – (A world of recipes)
    1. Cookery, Caribbean – Juvenile literature 2. Caribbean Area
    Description and travel – Juvenile literature
    I. Title
    641.5'123'09729

Acknowledgements
The Publishers would like to thank the following for permission to reproduce photographs:
Anthony Blake Photo Library, p.6; Robert Harding, p.5; All other photographs: Gareth Boden.
Illustration p.45, US Department of Agriculture/US Department of Health and Human Services.

Cover photographs reproduced with permission of Gareth Boden.

Our thanks to Sue Townsend, home economist, and Sue Mildenhall for their comments in the preparation of this book.

Every effort has been made to contact copyright holders of any material reproduced in this book. Any omissions will be rectified in subsequent printings if notice is given to the Publisher.

Words appearing in the text in bold, **like this**, are explained in the glossary.

Caribbean as slaves. The African people brought with them their own traditions and ways of cooking. At the end of the 19th century, slavery became illegal. The slaves left the sugar plantations and started their own farms. They grew different crops, such as cocoa and bananas.

▲ A sugar plantation on a Caribbean island.

Around the country

The climate varies between the different islands in the Caribbean. It is generally warm, but some islands are lush and green, while others are almost like deserts. Each area grows different crops. Coconuts, bananas, mangoes, oranges, limes, lemons, pineapples and papayas are common crops on many islands. On the desert-like islands, people use the local vegetables such as sweet potatoes, pumpkin, and even cactus, to create colourful and tasty meals.

Caribbean meals

A traditional Caribbean meal has three courses – a starter, a main course and a dessert. The starter might be vegetables or fruit made into a soup, or **deep-fried** and served with a salad. The main course is often a meat dish – usually chicken, pork or goat, often served with rice. Desserts are usually very sweet, and often include coconut or fruit.

Ingredients

sweet potato

pumpkin

mango

coconut

lime

banana

coconut milk

ginger

cinnamon

nutmeg

Many ingredients for Caribbean recipes are easy to find in supermarkets and shops.

Coconut

Coconuts grow all over the Caribbean, and are used in hundreds of different ways in Caribbean cooking. You can sometimes find fresh coconuts in shops and supermarkets. Blocks of creamed coconut and cans of coconut milk are easy to find as well. Coconut milk is made by grating the flesh of the coconut and mixing it with water. The **transparent** juice inside the coconut is a popular Caribbean drink, too.

Fruit

The climate of the Caribbean is ideal for growing all sorts of fruit. This book includes recipes that use some of the most common Caribbean fruits – bananas, mangoes and limes.

Plantains

Plantains are members of the banana family. They are bigger and firmer than bananas, and need to be cooked before they can be eaten. Plantains can be hard to find outside the Caribbean, so the recipes in this book use unripe, green bananas instead.

plantain

Pumpkin

Pumpkins are grown all over the Caribbean, and are a **staple** ingredient in many dishes, both sweet and savoury. If you can't find pumpkin, you can use any sort of squash, such as butternut squash, instead.

Spices

Spices are plants or seeds with strong flavours, which are used to add taste in cooking. Caribbean cooks use a lot of spices. Some of the most common are cinnamon, nutmeg, ginger, allspice and chilli powder. Chilli powder is very hot and spicy, so leave it out if you don't like spicy food. All of these spices can easily be bought dried, in jars or boxes.

Sweet potatoes

Sweet potatoes have orange or red skin, and orange flesh. They come from a different plant from ordinary potatoes, and are used in many Caribbean dishes.

Before you start

Kitchen rules

There are a few basic rules you should always follow when you are cooking.

- Ask an adult if you can use the kitchen.
- Some cooking processes, especially those involving hot water or oil, can be dangerous. When you see this sign, take extra care or ask an adult to help.
- Wash your hands before you start.
- Wear an apron to protect your clothes, and tie back long hair.
- Be very careful when you use sharp knives.
- Never leave pan handles sticking out in case you knock them.
- Always wear oven gloves to lift things in and out of the oven.
- Wash fruit and vegetables before you use them.

How long will it take?

Some of the recipes in this book are quick and easy, and some are more difficult and take longer. The strip across the top of the right hand page of each recipe tells you how long it takes to cook each dish from start to finish. It also shows how difficult each dish is to make: every recipe is either * (easy), ** (medium) or *** (difficult).

Quantities and measurements

You can see how many people each recipe will serve at the top of the right hand page, too. Most of the recipes in this book make enough to feed two people. Where it is more sensible to make a larger amount, though, the recipe makes enough for four.

You can multiply or divide the quantities if you want to cook for more or fewer people.

Ingredients for recipes can be measured in two different ways. Metric measurements use grams and millilitres. Imperial measurements use ounces and fluid ounces. This book uses metric measurements. If you want to convert these into imperial measurements, see the chart on page 44.

In the recipes you will see the following abbreviations:

tbsp = tablespoon   g = grams
tsp = teaspoon   ml = millilitres

Utensils

To cook the recipes in this book, you will need these utensils (as well as kitchen essentials such as spoons, plates and bowls):

- 2 baking tins (one 18cm round tin and one 900g loaf tin)
- chopping board
- cooling rack
- foil
- food processor or blender
- frying pan
- grater
- large bowl
- large, flat, ovenproof dish
- lemon squeezer
- measuring jug
- metal or wooden skewers
- roasting tin
- rolling pin
- saucepan with lid
- set of scales
- sharp knife
- sieve or colander
- small bowl
- wooden spoon

(!) Whenever you use kitchen knives, be very careful.

Pumpkin soup

What you need

1 garlic clove
½ onion
1kg fresh pumpkin
  (or use 500g canned
  pumpkin)
1 carrot
1 vegetable stock cube
1 tbsp sunflower oil
½ tsp chilli powder
  (optional)
¼ tsp dried ginger
¼ tsp cinnamon
¼ tsp allspice
400ml canned
  coconut milk
salt and pepper

Pumpkin is used in both savoury and sweet dishes in the Caribbean. Although pumpkin is actually a fruit, it is usually cooked like a vegetable.

What you do

1 **Peel** the skin from the garlic clove and the onion, and finely **chop** them.

2 If using fresh pumpkin, carefully cut it into quarters. Lay each quarter flat on a chopping board and carefully peel it as in this photo. Use a spoon to scoop out the seeds, and chop the pumpkin into bite-sized chunks.

3 Wash the carrot and chop it into pieces about the same size as the pumpkin chunks.

4 Put 500ml water into a saucepan, and bring it to the **boil**. Crumble the stock cube into the water, and stir it until it **dissolves**. Take the stock off the heat.

(!) **5** Heat the oil in a saucepan over a medium heat. Add the chopped onion, garlic and chilli powder (if using), and **fry** for 3 minutes.

6 Stir in the ginger, cinnamon, allspice, coconut milk, stock and a pinch of salt and pepper.

7 Bring the soup to the boil, then **simmer** it for 5 minutes. Add the chunks of carrot and the pumpkin, and bring the soup to the boil again.

8 **Cover** the pan, and cook the soup over a low heat for 40 minutes.

(!) **9** Carefully pour the hot soup into a food processor or blender, and **blend** it on the highest setting until it is smooth.

Banana soup

In the Caribbean, this soup is usually made with another member of the banana family, plantains. Plantains need to be cooked before they can be eaten, and can be hard to find. Bananas which are not yet completely ripe, and are still slightly green, make a good substitute in this dish.

What you need

2 unripe bananas
1 vegetable stock cube
250ml canned
    coconut milk
salt and pepper
¼ tsp chilli powder
    (optional)

What you do

1 Put 500ml water into a saucepan, and bring it to the **boil**. Crumble the stock cube into the water, and stir until it **dissolves**. Take the stock off the heat.

2 **Peel** the bananas, and cut them into thick **slices**.

3 Put the sliced bananas, stock, coconut milk, chilli powder (if using) and a pinch of salt and pepper into a saucepan.

4 Bring the soup to the boil, then **cover** the pan and cook the soup over a low heat for 10 minutes.

(!) 5 Pour the hot soup into a food processor or blender, and blend it on the highest setting until it is smooth.

SATURDAY SOUPS

Soup is popular on nearly all the Caribbean islands. It is often served on Saturday mornings, to use up leftovers before cooking a big Sunday lunch the next day.

Chicken and banana skewers

For this dish, pieces of chicken and banana are threaded onto sticks called skewers, and **grilled**. As with banana soup on page 12, this dish is often made with plantains in the Caribbean. This recipe uses unripe bananas, which are still slightly green.

What you need

1 tbsp smooth peanut butter
1 tsp paprika
¼ tsp dried ginger
1 chicken breast
2 unripe bananas

What you do

1 Put the peanut butter, paprika and ginger in a saucepan, and add 3 tbsp water. Heat gently over a low heat until the peanut butter has melted into the other ingredients. Pour the sauce into a bowl.

2 Cut the chicken into small pieces. Put the chicken pieces into the bowl with the sauce, and mix well so the chicken is coated with the sauce. Leave it to **marinate** in the sauce for 1 hour.

3 **Peel** the bananas, and cut them into thick **slices**.

4 Take the chicken pieces out of the sauce. Push a piece of chicken, then a piece of banana onto a skewer until it is full. Then make three more.

5 Brush the skewered chicken and banana with the left-over sauce.

6 Grill the skewered chicken and banana under a medium grill for 10 minutes, turning halfway through, until they are golden brown on the outside and the chicken is white on the inside.

VEGETARIAN VARIATION

Try making vegetarian skewers by replacing the chicken with pieces of pumpkin or sweet potato. Cut the vegetables into pieces, and **boil** them in water for 10 minutes before marinating them in the same way as the chicken.

Chicken in coconut sauce

Coconuts grow on most Caribbean islands, and are used in many dishes. Both their flesh and their milk are very **nutritious**. In this dish, coconut milk makes a creamy sauce for the chicken.

What you need

2 chicken breasts
1 garlic clove
½ onion
2 spring onions
1 tbsp sunflower oil
¼ tsp chilli powder
  (optional)
¼ tsp curry powder
½ tsp dried thyme
300ml canned
  coconut milk

What you do

1 Chop the chicken breasts into small pieces.

2 Peel the skin from the garlic clove and onion, and finely chop them.

3 Cut the tops and bottoms off the spring onions, and finely chop them.

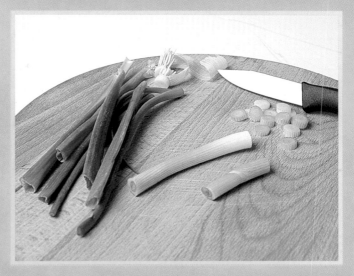

4 Heat the oil in a saucepan. Add the chicken pieces, chopped garlic, onion, chilli powder (if using) and curry powder.

5 Fry the mixture for 10 minutes, stirring occasionally.

6 Add the chopped spring onions, thyme and coconut milk to the saucepan.

7 Bring the mixture to the **boil**, then reduce the heat and **simmer** for about 40 minutes, until the sauce has thickened.

8 Serve with plain boiled rice.

Cod and prawn bake

The sea around the Caribbean islands provides the people with lots of fish. This recipe makes enough to feed four people, served with boiled rice. You can use fresh or frozen cod – if using frozen, make sure you move it from the freezer to the fridge about 12 hours before you start cooking, so it is completely **thawed**.

What you need

2 garlic cloves
2 onions
1 aubergine
4 medium potatoes
150g cabbage
240g pumpkin
4 cod fillets
100ml olive oil
½ tsp chilli powder
   (optional)
30g fresh parsley
240g peeled prawns

What you do

1 **Preheat** the oven to 190°C/375°F/gas mark 5.

2 **Peel** the skin from the garlic cloves and onions, and finely **chop** them.

3 Chop the aubergine into pieces about 1cm across.

4 Peel or scrub the potatoes, and cut them into thin **slices**.

5 Finely **shred** the cabbage.

6 Peel the skin from the pumpkin, remove the seeds, and cut it into pieces about 1cm across.

7 Finely chop the parsley.

8 Put the fish into a saucepan. Cover it with water, bring to the **boil** and then **simmer** for about 5 minutes.

⚠ **9** **Drain** the fish. **Flake** it into a bowl, removing any skin and bones.

⚠ **10** Heat half the olive oil in a saucepan over a low heat. Add the chopped onion, garlic, aubergine and chilli powder (if using). **Fry** for 10 minutes, until the aubergine is soft.

11 Add the flaked fish to the onion and aubergine mixture, and mix together well.

12 In this order, spoon a layer of each ingredient into an ovenproof dish:
- potato slices
- fish and onion mixture
- shredded cabbage
- prawns
- chopped pumpkin
- parsley

13 **Drizzle** the rest of the oil over the top of the dish. **Cover** it with foil, and **bake** for 30 minutes.

14 Remove the foil, and bake for a further 20 minutes.

19

Baked fish with lime and orange juice

You can use all sorts of different fish in this recipe. It is often cooked with red snapper in the Caribbean, but if you can't get hold of any, try using fresh or frozen cod or haddock. If you use frozen fish, move it from the freezer to the fridge about 12 hours before you start cooking so it is completely **thawed**.

What you need

2 garlic cloves
½ onion
2 spring onions
2 limes
1 orange
2 fish fillets
½ tsp sugar
½ tsp dried thyme
¼ tsp chilli powder
    (optional)
salt and pepper

What you do

1 **Preheat** the oven to 200°C/ 400°F/gas mark 6.

2 **Peel** the skin from the garlic clove and onion and finely **chop** them.

3 Cut the tops and bottoms off the spring onions and finely chop them.

4 Cut the limes and orange in half. Squeeze the juice out of them with a lemon squeezer.

5 Put the fish fillets into an ovenproof dish. Pour 200ml water around them.

6 Pour the lime and orange juice over the fish.

7 Put the chopped garlic, sugar, thyme, chopped onion, chopped spring onions, chilli powder (if using) and a pinch of salt and pepper onto the fish.

8 **Cover** the dish with foil, and **bake** the fish for 30 minutes. Serve it with plain boiled rice.

RED SNAPPER

Red snapper is one of the most popular fish in the Caribbean. It is the most common species of snapper, but other species come in all sorts of different colours and patterns, including stripy snapper!

Baked 'ground provisions'

The term 'ground provisions' is used to describe vegetables that are grown all over the Caribbean, like sweet potatoes and pumpkins. It suggests using food that the ground provides.

What you need

400ml canned
  coconut milk
150g potatoes
150g sweet potatoes
150g pumpkin
100g hard cheese, for
  example Cheddar
15g butter or
  margarine
15g cornflour

What you do

1 **Preheat** the oven to 180°C/ 350°F/gas mark 4.

2 Cut the pumpkin into quarters and **peel** them. Scoop out the seeds, and cut the pumpkin into thin **slices**.

3 Peel the potatoes and sweet potatoes, and cut them into thin slices.

4 Put the coconut milk into a saucepan, and bring it to the **boil**. Add the sliced potatoes, sweet potatoes and pumpkin.

5 **Simmer** the vegetables in the coconut milk for 10 minutes.

6 **Drain** the coconut milk from the vegetables into a bowl. Put it to one side.

7 **Grate** the cheese into a bowl.

8 Melt the butter or margarine in a saucepan over a low heat.

9 Take the saucepan off the heat, and gradually add the cornflour, stirring all the time, to make a thick paste.

10 Still keeping the pan off the heat, slowly stir the coconut milk into the paste.

11 Put the sauce back onto the heat, and heat gradually, stirring all the time, until it becomes thick and starts to bubble. Stir in the grated cheese and cook for another minute until all the cheese has melted.

12 Arrange the slices of potato, sweet potato and pumpkin in an ovenproof dish. Pour the cheese sauce over the top.

13 **Bake** in the oven, uncovered, for 25 minutes.

Banana curry

As with banana soup (page 12), and chicken and banana skewers (page 14), this dish is usually made with plantains in the Caribbean. If you can find them, cook them in the same way as the bananas in this recipe. If you can't, use unripe bananas, which are still slightly green, instead. Serve your curry with plain, boiled rice.

What you need

15g butter or
    margarine
15g cornflour
1 tsp curry powder
400ml canned
    coconut milk
¼ tsp nutmeg
2 unripe bananas (or
    plantains if possible)
salt and pepper

What you do

1 **Preheat** the oven to 230°C/ 450°F/gas mark 8.

2 Melt the butter or margarine in a saucepan over a low heat. When it is melted, take the saucepan off the heat, and gradually add the cornflour, stirring all the time, to make a thick paste.

3 Still keeping the pan off the heat, gradually stir the coconut milk into the paste. Do this very slowly so you don't get lumps in the sauce.

4 Put the sauce back on to the heat, and heat gradually, stirring all the time, until it becomes thick and starts to bubble.

5 Add the nutmeg, curry powder and a pinch of salt and pepper to the sauce, and stir.

6 **Peel** the bananas and cut them into thick **slices**. Arrange them in the bottom of an ovenproof dish.

7 Pour the sauce over the bananas.

8 **Bake** your curry in the oven, uncovered, for 30 minutes.

PLANTAIN CRISPS

Plantains can be **fried**, **boiled** or baked. Plantain crisps (a bit like potato crisps) are made by cutting plantains into thin slices, then **deep-frying** them and sprinkling them with salt.

Bean and egg salad

Caribbean cooks use many types of beans. Beans are filling and **nutritious**. This salad contains three different types – kidney beans, haricot beans and green beans. You could eat this salad as a main course, perhaps with some crusty bread.

What you need

1 red onion
2 tbsp olive oil
1 tbsp balsamic
  vinegar or red wine
  vinegar
1 tbsp mayonnaise
200g canned kidney
  beans
200g canned haricot
  beans
300g green beans
2 or 3 large lettuce
  leaves
2 eggs

What you do

1 **Peel** the skin from the onion and finely **chop** it.

2 In a bowl, mix together the oil, vinegar and mayonnaise.

3 Add the chopped onion, **drained** kidney beans and drained haricot beans to the mixture.

4 Cut the ends off the green beans. If they are long, cut them in half. Bring a saucepan of water to the **boil**, and add the green beans to the pan. Boil them for 5 minutes, then drain the water from the beans and leave them to **cool**.

5 Using a spoon, carefully lower the eggs into a saucepan. Add enough water to cover them.

6 Bring the water to the boil, then reduce the heat and **simmer** the eggs for 8 minutes.

7 Use a spoon to lift the eggs out of the water. Hold them under the cold tap to cool them, then peel off the shells.

8 Put the lettuce leaves on a plate. Put the kidney and haricot bean mixture in the middle of the lettuce leaves.

9 Arrange the green beans in a circle around the bean mixture. Cut the eggs into **slices**, and arrange these in a circle around the green beans.

Red, yellow and green salad

This colourful and refreshing salad is ideal for a hot day. It could be served as a side dish, or you could eat it with crusty bread as a snack or light lunch.

What you need

1 green pepper
1 yellow pepper
1 red pepper
2 large tomatoes
½ lettuce (for example iceberg, or cos)
1 lime
3 tbsp olive oil
½ tbsp white wine vinegar
¼ tsp paprika
¼ tsp sugar
salt and pepper

What you do

1 Cut the tops off the peppers, and scoop out the seeds. Cut the peppers into round **slices**.

2 Cut the tomatoes into thin slices.

3 **Shred** the lettuce.

4 Arrange the salad in a bowl in layers. Put a layer of green peppers at the bottom, followed by a layer of tomatoes, a layer of yellow peppers and a layer of red peppers.

5 Top the salad with the shredded lettuce.

6 Cut the lime in half. Using a lemon squeezer, squeeze the juice out of one half of it.

7 Put the lime juice, olive oil, vinegar, paprika, sugar and a pinch of salt and pepper into a small bowl, and mix them together well to make a dressing for the salad.

8 **Drizzle** the dressing evenly over the salad. Try not to mix it in, or you will spoil the layers you have built up.

SERVING THE SALAD

If you can, make this salad in a glass bowl, so you can see the different layers through the side of the bowl. When you serve it, use a knife to cut it into colourful 'wedges'.

Coconut custard

Coconuts are used in many Caribbean dishes. The name 'coconut' comes from a Portuguese word meaning 'monkey's face'. Perhaps the 15th century Portuguese explorers who sailed to the Caribbean thought the three dents on a coconut shell looked like a monkey's face! You need to make this custard a few hours before you want to eat it, as it needs time to **chill**.

What you need

100ml single cream
2 eggs
25g caster sugar
100ml canned
    coconut milk
½ tsp vanilla essence

What you do

1 **Preheat** the oven to 165°C/ 325°F/gas mark 3.

2 Put the cream, eggs and sugar into a food processor or blender. **Blend** the ingredients on the highest setting until they make a smooth paste.

3 Add the coconut milk and vanilla essence to the mixture, and blend together for a few seconds.

(!) 4 Pour the mixture into an ovenproof bowl. Put the bowl into a roasting tin, and carefully pour hot water into the tin so that the water comes halfway up the sides of the bowl. **Cover** the whole roasting tin with foil.

5 Carefully put the roasting tin into the oven and cook the custard for 1 hour.

6 Take it out of the oven and leave it to **cool** for a couple of hours. When it is cold, put it into the fridge to chill.

COCONUT JUICE

Coconut juice is the **transparent** liquid which forms in the middle of a coconut. It is sold on street stalls all over the Caribbean. The coconut juice seller cuts off the top of the coconut with a knife or an axe, then sticks a straw into the hole before handing the coconut to the thirsty customer!

Sweet potato and pumpkin pudding

Sweet potatoes and pumpkins are used in both savoury and sweet Caribbean dishes. This dessert combines sweet potato and pumpkin with spices and dried fruit.

What you need

200g sweet potatoes
200g pumpkin
1 tsp dried ginger
½ tsp nutmeg
½ tsp cinnamon
½ tsp vanilla essence
50g raisins
100ml canned
    coconut milk
50g brown sugar
10g butter or
    margarine

What you do

1 **Preheat** the oven to 200°C/400°F/gas mark 6.

2 **Peel** the sweet potatoes and the pumpkin. **Grate** both of them into a bowl.

3 Add the ginger, nutmeg, cinnamon, vanilla essence and raisins to the bowl of grated sweet potatoes and pumpkin.

4 Melt the butter or margarine in a saucepan.

5 In a bowl, mix together the coconut milk, sugar and melted butter or margarine. Pour this mixture into the sweet potato and pumpkin mixture, and stir everything together.

6 Using your fingers, rub some extra butter or margarine into an 18cm round baking tin.

7 Spoon the pudding mixture into the baking tin. **Bake** it in the oven for 1½ hours.

8 Take the pudding out of the oven, and let it stand for 10 minutes before serving.

Banana bread

Banana bread is cooked all over the Caribbean. You could eat it as a pudding with cream, or as a snack. It is best to use very ripe bananas.

What you need

100g butter or
  margarine
250g brown sugar
1 egg
3 ripe bananas
350g self-raising flour
½ tsp cinnamon
½ tsp nutmeg
100ml milk
1 tsp vanilla essence

What you do

1 **Preheat** the oven to 180°C/ 350°F/gas mark 4.

2 **Peel** the bananas, and, using a fork, **mash** them in a bowl.

3 Using a wooden spoon, **beat** the butter and sugar together in a bowl. Add the egg, and beat the mixture for 1 minute.

4 Add the mashed bananas to the butter, sugar and egg mixture, and mix everything together.

5 Using a metal spoon, **fold** the flour, cinnamon and nutmeg into the mixture.

6 Add the milk and vanilla essence to the mixture. Stir the mixture well.

7 Using your fingers, rub some butter or margarine into a 900g loaf tin.

8 Spoon the banana bread mixture into the loaf tin. **Bake** it in the oven for 1 hour.

9 Using an oven glove, tip it out onto a cooling rack to **cool** before you slice it.

IS IT COOKED?

You can check whether the banana bread is cooked by sticking a skewer or a sharp knife straight down into the middle of the bread. If the skewer comes out clean, the bread is ready. If it comes out with some mixture stuck to it, put the bread back in the oven for a few more minutes.

Pancakes with mangoes

You need a really ripe mango for this dish. Check if it is ripe by squeezing it gently – if you feel it 'give', it is ripe.

What you need

1 ripe mango
1 tbsp caster sugar
1 egg
175ml milk
80g plain flour
½ tsp nutmeg
2 tbsp sunflower oil

What you do

1 **Peel** the skin from the mango. Cut the flesh from either side of the flat stone.

2 Put the mango flesh into a food processor or blender with the caster sugar. **Blend** the mango on the highest setting until it becomes a **pulp**.

3 Spoon the mango pulp into a bowl, then clean the blender.

4 Put the egg and milk into the blender and turn it to its highest setting for about 30 seconds.

5 Turn the blender to low, and gradually pour in the flour, then add the nutmeg. Blend the batter until it is smooth.

6 Put the batter into the fridge, and leave it to stand for 30 minutes.

(!) 7 Heat ½ tbsp oil in a medium-sized non-stick frying pan over a medium heat. Put 3 tbsp of the pancake batter into the pan, and swirl it around so that the batter spreads out.

8 Cook the pancake for about 1 minute, then turn it over and cook the other side for the same time.

9 Slide the pancake out of the pan onto a plate, and repeat steps 7 and 8 until you have made four pancakes.

10 Divide the mango pulp between the four pancakes, spreading it over half of the pancake.

11 Fold the other half of the pancake over the top of the filling, and fold the pancake again.

37

Mango ice cream

It can get very hot in the Caribbean, so ice cream is popular. To make this recipe, you need really ripe mangoes – see page 36 for how to check whether a mango is ripe. This recipe makes enough for four.

What you need

2 ripe mangoes
300ml milk
4 egg yolks
100g caster sugar
300ml double cream

What you do

1 **Peel** the skin from the mangoes. Cut the flesh from the stone, and put the flesh into a food processor or blender. **Blend** the mango on the highest setting until it becomes a **pulp**.

2 Put the milk into a saucepan. Heat it until it is hot, but not **boiling**.

3 To separate the egg yolks from the whites, carefully crack the egg. Keeping the yolk in one half of the shell, let the white drip into a bowl. Pass the yolk from one half of the shell to the other until all the white has dripped out. Put the yolk in a separate bowl. Do this for all four eggs.
Beat the egg yolks and sugar together in a bowl until they are well mixed.

(!) **4** Gradually stir the hot milk into the egg and sugar mixture, stirring all the time.

5 Pour the mixture back into the saucepan. Cook it over a low heat until it thickens (this should take about 10 minutes).

6 Pour the mixture into a bowl, then **whisk** in the cream and the pulped mango.

7 Put the mixture into the freezer. After an hour, take the bowl out of the freezer, and **mash** the mixture with a fork to break up any lumps.

8 Repeat step 7 until the ice cream is set. This should take about 4 or 5 hours, depending on how cold your freezer is.

Ginger beer

Ginger beer is drunk all over the Caribbean. It is often sold on street stalls. Each stall has a huge block of ice, and the ginger beer seller chips some ice off the block, puts it into a cup, then pours the ginger beer over the top to make a wonderfully cool and refreshing drink.

Although ginger beer is quick and easy to make, you have to leave it to stand for a couple of days so that the taste of the ginger spreads through the whole drink.

What you need

large piece fresh
    ginger (about 30g)
175g caster sugar

What you do

1 **Peel** the skin from the ginger, then **grate** the ginger finely. Keep your fingers clear!

2 Put 1½ litres water into a large saucepan, and bring it to the **boil**.

3 Add the grated ginger and caster sugar to the boiling water. Stir everything together, then turn off the heat.

4 Put a lid on the pan, and leave it to stand somewhere cool for a couple of days.

5 Pour the ginger beer through a sieve into a jug, then pour it into a plastic or glass bottle.

6 Keep the bottle in the fridge until you want to drink the ginger beer.

GINGER MEDICINE

Ginger is used by many people as a medicine.
In the Caribbean, a hot drink made from ginger is
used to relieve stomach pains and flu.

Coconut milkshake

Coconuts are used in many ways in Caribbean life. The flesh of the coconut is an ingredient in lots of different dishes. The liquid in the middle of the coconut is drunk (see box on page 31). The coconut shell is turned into utensils such as spoons and cups, and the leaves of the coconut tree are used to make roofs for houses.

This coconut milkshake is refreshing and easy to make.

What you need

200ml vanilla ice
    cream
200ml canned
    coconut milk
100ml milk
½ tsp nutmeg

What you do

1 Put all the ingredients into a food processor or blender.

2 **Blend** the milkshake on the highest setting until it is smooth.

3 Pour the milkshake into two glasses. That's it!

OTHER MILKSHAKES

You can make milkshakes in all sorts of different flavours. Try replacing the coconut milk with mashed bananas or strawberries, or with cold, sweet, black coffee.

ADDING ICE

To make your milkshakes even more refreshing on a hot day, put ice cubes in the bottom of the glasses before pouring in the milkshake.

43

Further information

Here are some places to find out more about the Caribbean and its cooking.

Books

Cooking the Caribbean Way
Cheryl Davidson Kaufman, Lerner Publications, 1989
Exploring Caribbean Food in Britain
Floella Benjamin, Mantra, 1988
Flavours of the Caribbean
Linda Illsley, Hodder Wayland, 1998
Caribbean Home Economics
Gill Veda, Heinemann, 1993

Websites

soar.berkeley.edu/recipes/ethnic/caribbean
www.ajlc.waterloo.on.ca/Recipes/Caribbean
www.astray.com/recipes/?search=caribbean
www.caribcon.com/caribkit.html
www.globalgourmet.com/destinations/caribbean
www.yumyum.com/recipes/htm

Conversion chart

Ingredients for recipes can be measured in two different ways. Metric measurements use grams and millilitres. Imperial measurements use ounces and fluid ounces. This book uses metric measurements. The chart here shows you how to convert measurements from metric to imperial.

SOLIDS		LIQUIDS	
METRIC	IMPERIAL	METRIC	IMPERIAL
10g	¼ oz	30ml	1 fl oz
15g	½ oz	50ml	2 fl oz
25g	1 oz	75ml	2½ fl oz
50g	1¾ oz	100ml	3½ fl oz
75g	2¾ oz	125ml	4 fl oz
100g	3½ oz	150ml	5 fl oz
150g	5 oz	300ml	10 fl oz
250g	9 oz	600ml	20 fl oz

Healthy eating

This diagram shows which foods you should eat to stay healthy. Most of your food should come from the bottom of the pyramid. Eat some of the foods from the middle every day. Only eat a little of the foods from the top.

Healthy eating, Caribbean style

Caribbean cooking uses many ingredients from the bottom of the pyramid – for example people often eat rice as part of their main meal. The rest of the meal might consist of chicken, or fish, or beans, along with vegetables such as pumpkin, plaintains or peppers. Coconut is used in sauces and desserts, so you can see how healthy caribbean cooking is!

Fats, oils, cakes and sweets

KEY
◻ Fat   ◸ Sugars

Milk, yoghurt, and cheese

Meat, poultry, fish, dry beans, eggs and nuts

Vegetables

Fruit

Breads, cereal, rice and pasta

Glossary

bake cook something in the oven

beat mix something together strongly, for example egg yolks and whites

blend mix ingredients together in a blender or food processor

boil cook a liquid on the hob. Boiling liquid bubbles and steams strongly.

chill put something in the fridge to make it cold before serving it

chop cut something into pieces using a knife

cool allow hot food to become cold. You should always allow food to cool before putting it in the fridge.

cover put a lid on a pan, or foil over a dish

deep-fried cooked in deep, hot oil

dissolve mix something into a liquid until it disappears

drain remove liquid, usually by pouring something into a colander or sieve

drizzle pour something very slowly and evenly

flake break something, for example a piece of fish, into small pieces

fold mix ingredients together very slowly and carefully

fry cook something in oil in a pan

grate break something, for example cheese, into small pieces using a grater

grill cook something under the grill

marinate soak something, such as meat or fish, in a mixture before cooking, so that it absorbs the taste of the mixture

mash crush something, for example potato, until it is soft and pulpy

nutritious good, healthy food to eat

peel remove the skin of a fruit or vegetable

preheat turn on the oven in advance, so that it is hot when you are ready to use it

pulp a mixture that has been mashed or blended until smooth

shred cut or tear something, for example a lettuce, into small pieces

simmer cook a liquid on the hob. Simmering liquid bubbles and steams gently.

slice cut something into thin, flat pieces

staple a main ingredient, one found in many dishes

thaw defrost something which has been frozen

transparent see-through

whisk mix ingredients using a whisk

Index